Original title:
The Mango Dreamer

Copyright © 2025 Creative Arts Management OÜ
All rights reserved.

Author: Gideon Shaw
ISBN HARDBACK: 978-1-80586-424-0
ISBN PAPERBACK: 978-1-80586-896-5

Lush Fantasies

In a grove where laughter flows,
Mangoes dance with breezy prose.
Silly thoughts in sunlit haze,
Creating joy on lazy days.

Birds wear hats of fruity hue,
Sipping smoothies, feeling new.
Bouncing squirrels throw mango balls,
While chipmunks sing in garden halls.

Beneath the shade, old turtles swim,
Pranking frogs on a mango whim.
A picnic spreads with snacks galore,
As friends just giggle, crave for more.

The Fruit of Imagination

In dreams where fruits and jokes collide,
The mango rides a silly slide.
With jelly beans and peanut flies,
They race beneath the sunny skies.

Bananas slip and giggle loud,
A wobbly, dancing, fruit-filled crowd.
Grapes throw shade and dare to weave,
While twirly pears just laugh and leave.

Each slice a piece of funny cheer,
In fruity realms where jokes adhere.
Mango moons up in the night,
As laughter glows, a pure delight.

Nectar of the Night

Under starry skies so bright,
Mangoes glow, a funny sight.
Lively jokes in every squeeze,
As fireflies join in the tease.

With sassy swirls of party flair,
A silly dance, no one would dare.
Fruits giggle in a blender spin,
Crafting smoothies thick with whim.

The midnight feast a comical cheer,
With jokes that only fruits can hear.
A splash of humor, laughter's kiss,
In nectar's pool, we find our bliss.

Tranquil Harvest

In fields where fruits glimmer and glow,
Comical tales begin to flow.
Harvest dances soft and bright,
Mango dreams take playful flight.

Bumbling bees all dressed in gold,
Share their fun, the stories told.
With every pick, a chuckle shared,
In orchards where none are scared.

A tranquil breeze, the laughter flies,
With fruity giggles in the skies.
Mangoes smile in evening's grace,
As humor finds its happy place.

Bags of Dreamy Delights

In bags of joy so round and bright,
Contemplating flavors, a pure delight.
Sitting with friends, laughter flows,
While munching snacks, our happiness grows.

With puns and jokes, we share our treats,
Citrus giggles and zesty beats.
Tasting the sunshine, a curious blend,
In each fruity bite, our smiles extend.

The pit's a riddle, what's hidden inside?
A world of fun, we giggle and hide.
Joyful moments, wrapped up tight,
In bags of sweetness, everything's right.

Picking Golden Moments

Under the trees, the sun shines bright,
Reaching for laughter, oh what a sight!
With every pluck, new joy is found,
Golden treasures scattered around.

A splash of nectar, a tickle of zing,
Life's silly melodies dance and sing.
Each chosen piece, a story we weave,
In our merry quest, we truly believe.

Friends by our side, we feast and play,
Nibbling on dreams that brighten the day.
In every bite, a joke or two,
As we relish the moments, fresh and new.

Tropical Whispers

Tropical breezes carry our cheer,
With whispers of joy, we hold dear.
Palm trees sway to the comic tune,
As shadows dance beneath the moon.

A splash of color, a twist of fate,
Each fruity mouthful cannot wait.
With giggles popping, a fruity spree,
In this lively land, we feel so free.

A joke from a friend, a joke from a fruit,
Giggles and crunch, oh what a hoot!
With every slice, a laugh we share,
In tropical lands, silly without care.

Slices of Sunlight

Slices of sunshine, so juicy and sweet,
A burst of laughter in every treat.
Chomping away, we giggle and sigh,
As flavors dance, we reach for the sky.

In each little nibble, stories unfold,
With secrets and chuckles our friendship holds.
Golden happiness on a whimsical plate,
Slices of fortune we truly appreciate.

As we gather 'round, the jokes take flight,
Tasting the day, everything feels right.
With every crunch, we weave our dreams,
In this vibrant world, nothing's as it seems.

Beneath the Mango Tree

Beneath the boughs, a laughter grows,
Where fruit like suns in green light glows.
A parrot squawks, in jokes he's steeped,
As mangoes drop, while giggles creep.

Sipping juice, a sticky fate,
A dance of flies, no time to wait.
With every bite, a story spills,
Of fruity dreams and sunlit thrills.

Friends gather round, with grins so wide,
As mango juice drips, no place to hide.
We chase the seeds, they bounce and roll,
In this sweet place, we find our soul.

So here we sit, in gleeful cheer,
With golden bites and plenty of beer.
The mangoes tease, they play their game,
And in this joy, we all feel fame.

Golden Fruits of Fantasy

In dreams of gold, a mango band,
With every bite, we take a stand.
The shades of yellow, like a crown,
We're kings and queens of juicy town.

Adventures start with one big toss,
A mango fight? A real big loss!
The juice erupts, a sweet surprise,
With laughter loud, we touch the skies.

Three pieces left, and jokes ignite,
A dance-off starts, oh what a sight!
With sticky hands and crazy feet,
We whirl around, let's take a seat.

In this wild realm of fruity glee,
The world's a stage, come dance with me.
The golden fruits, they sparkle bright,
In every laugh, we find delight.

Sweetness in the Breeze

A gentle breeze, a magical ride,
As mangoes sway, we laugh and glide.
With every gust, they hit the ground,
And sticky chins are all around.

The summer sun has got a plan,
A feast awaits, come join the clan.
With shirts all stained and taste buds wild,
We're just like kids, all gleefully styled.

A mango pit, oh what a toss,
Aiming for the pond, what a loss!
We giggle loud, the splash is grand,
Our summer games, they're simply planned.

And as the day sinks in delight,
With juicy smiles, we end the night.
The breeze still sings its fruity sound,
In this sweet world, we dance around.

Echoes of the Summer Sky

Underneath the sun's warm cling,
Echoes of laughter, a happy ring.
Mangoes roll like treasures divine,
As we chase joy in every line.

In silly hats, we take our stand,
With juice in hand, we make a band.
A conga line of laughter flows,
With every jump, the magic grows.

The clouds above, they wink and sway,
As fruit-filled jokes light up the day.
We toss the pits like shooting stars,
Laughing loud, like rock'n'roll guitars.

So let the echoes fill the air,
With joyful tales, we've got to share.
For in this space, where fun's the prize,
We find sweet treasures under the skies.

Hues of Gold and Green

In a world of colors bright,
Gold and green, a silly sight.
Fruits that dance in happy cheer,
Whisper tales for all to hear.

Chasing dreams on branches high,
With each leap, a funny sigh.
Fruits that wink with cheeky charm,
Causing giggles, spreading warm.

Taste of Sunlit Memories

A splash of joy upon my tongue,
Flavors burst, and laughter's sung.
Sunlit joys that make me grin,
Sweet and tangy, here we begin.

In every bite, a joke revealed,
Taste of fun, my fate is sealed.
Memories ripe, a fruity jest,
Fill my heart with zest of zest.

The Orchard's Secret

Hidden gems in leafy halls,
Whispers, laughter, fruit ball calls.
Squirrels giggle, fruits collide,
Nature's humor, can't divide.

Tickling leaves in playful tease,
Yummy laughter floats in the breeze.
Secrets shared in fruit-filled chats,
Funny tales of cheeky bats.

Tropical Essence

In the tropics, colors play,
Essence brightens up the day.
Funky fruits in wild parade,
Spreading joy that won't fade.

Bouncing beats of nature's tune,
Tickling feet beneath the moon.
Coconut chuckles, pineapple pranks,
Tropical laughter fills the ranks.

Tropical Whispers

In a land where the sun does play,
Fruits giggle in a colorful ballet.
Bananas wear hats, quite divine,
While coconuts sip on coconut wine.

Lime rolls by with a cheeky grin,
He says, 'Join me, let the fun begin!'
Mangoes laugh under the laughing tree,
"Who knew fruit could be so carefree?"

Pineapples dance with knock-kneed flair,
While strawberries wiggle without a care.
Citrus charms the birds in flight,
Spreading joy from morning's light.

Underneath the palm's soft sway,
We frolic, hop, and sing away.
With vibrant hues and laughter bright,
Tropical pals bring pure delight.

Sunlit Reflections

A mango spins in a sunbeam's glow,
Chasing shadows with a playful throw.
"Catch me if you can," it shouts with glee,
As fruit flies laugh in a fruity spree.

Ripened gems of orange and red,
Giggle together like kids, well-fed.
Coconut drummers beat a tune,
While Pineapple swings like a cartoon.

Juicy splashes on a sunny day,
Watermelon diving in a big display.
"We're the stars of this sunny scene!"
As laughter echoes, bright and keen.

With rays that dance on laughter's wings,
Fruity folks make the best of things.
In a whirl of joy and flavors sweet,
Life's a festival; let's move our feet!

Juicy Reveries

In a garden bursting with cheer,
Peaches whisper, "Hey, come near!"
"Join our party, it's quite a blast,
Where every moment's a fruity feast!"

Lemons tossed are bright and zesty,
While kiwis giggle, feeling testy.
Raspberry pies take a silly bow,
As laughter bursts from every row.

Plum hopscotch around in delight,
Making fruit salad thoughts take flight.
"Who says we're just for eating, friend?
We're a joke book with a fruity blend!"

Sunset hues paint the sky aglow,
Mischief brews like a fruity show.
With smiles abound and joy declared,
In this orchard, laughter's shared.

Dreams of the Orchard

Under an arch of leafy sway,
Comical fruits laugh the day away.
A bouncing melon, spry and bright,
Challenges the sun to a playful fight.

Grapes rolling in a playful spree,
Whisper secrets to the honeybee.
"Let's make a game, let's make a scene,
Where every fruit gets to be a queen!"

Berries jest about their roundness,
Waving to the world with such fondness.
Oranges clap with zestful cheer,
While cherries giggle without fear.

Dreams twirl in this fragrant land,
Where fruit can dance, and we can't stand.
In the orchard's light, so warm and bold,
Life's a comedy just waiting to unfold.

Blossoms Beneath a Sapphire Sky

In a garden bright with glee,
A tree danced just for me,
Its fruits hung low, a tasty tease,
I reached up high, with such a breeze.

Butterflies in colors bold,
Sipped nectar, tales untold,
A squirrel grinned, quite a delight,
Joined the fun, what a sight!

Laughter echoed, birds did sing,
While I dreamed of fruity bling,
Swirling thoughts like candy twists,
In this paradise, nothing missed.

With each bite, a giggle spun,
Juicy drips, oh what fun!
A silly smile upon my face,
In the sun, I found my place.

Enchanted by Citrus Light

Under rays so bright and warm,
Lemon laughs, a fruity charm,
Each slice of laughter, zest so bold,
In this grove, sweet tales unfold.

An orange danced alongside me,
With jokes that buzzed like honey bee,
A tango with a twisty lime,
Each moment ripe, each quip sublime.

The peels were hats, we wore with pride,
As we waddled side by side,
Fruit friends in a merry line,
Cooking up a punch so fine.

We juggled fruit and sang some tunes,
Beneath the light of smiling moons,
In this citrus-fueled delight,
Joy held tight, oh what a sight!

Serenity in Golden Lights

Golden rays through leafy green,
Brought a glow, bright and keen,
Bananas giggled, swayed with ease,
In the breeze, they aimed to please.

Cherries chuckled, red and round,
In this orchard, joy abounds,
With each swing and sway, they cheered,
For the moments we all steered.

A pear did leap, and off it went,
A tumble that was heaven-sent,
Rolling round with such a flair,
With laughter lightening every care.

In this dream of fruity fun,
Friendship forged beneath the sun,
With giggles ripe and silly sights,
Life's a laugh, in golden lights.

Tales of the Sunlit Grove

In the grove where shadows play,
Each fruit had something small to say,
An apple winked, a peach would grin,
While grapes gossiped, where to begin?

A coconut spun on its head,
Knocking jokes 'til daylight fled,
With laughter bouncing off the trees,
Sunny whispers danced with ease.

The figs told tales from days gone by,
Of fruit fights under the open sky,
Together we rolled, a merry throng,
Creating a world where we belong.

In the sunlit, cheerful frame,
Life's a game, a silly game,
With stories woven into the air,
In this grove, our hearts laid bare.

Palm Tree Serenade

Under palm trees, I sway,
Dreaming of fruit so bright,
Falling coconuts in play,
I dodge them left and right.

Banana peels on my way,
Oh, what a slippery scene!
Chasing dreams of sunny ray,
I slip, I laugh, I'm keen.

Lemonade spills in the sand,
With laughter in the air,
Friends join in, a joyful band,
In summer's vibrant glare.

Tropical breezes invite,
As we dance in the light,
With a wink and a bite,
Life's just a funny sight.

Colorful Daydreams

In a world of vibrant hues,
Cherries giggle, berries sing,
Mangoes wear their finest shoes,
As butterflies take wing.

Watermelons roll around,
Cracking jokes with each big splash,
A fruit fiesta brightly found,
We all join in the bash.

Grapes gossip under the vine,
Peaches blush, they look so sweet,
Laughter flows like sparkling wine,
Every bite a tasty treat.

In this carnival of fruit,
Life's a game, a merry dance,
Join the fun, take a hoot,
In these colorful expanse.

Sunlit Reflections

Beneath the sun, shadows play,
Goofy smiles all around,
Sunshine sparkles, bright as day,
Where silly antics abound.

Juggling fruits, a comical show,
Tumbling lemons, apples too,
Laughing loud, let mischief flow,
Each moment, something new.

The pool's a splash of joy,
Rubber ducks quack with glee,
Silly games we all enjoy,
Floating in a fruity sea.

With whispers of summer breeze,
Life's a giggle, never meek,
Funny moments aim to please,
In the sun's embrace, we speak.

The Dance of Ripe Delights

Fruits frolic on the stage,
Cherries twirl, bananas glide,
Laughter joins this fruity page,
As joy spills side to side.

Avocados show some flair,
Doing flips in perfect time,
Coconuts roll everywhere,
Creating a hilarious rhyme.

Pineapples don party hats,
Strutting like they own the crowd,
Mangoes dance with silly chats,
Every moment, bright and loud.

In the groove, the rhythm sways,
With a wink, we leap and dive,
In this fruit-filled, fun-filled maze,
Together, we come alive.

Vivid Slices of Summer

In a world of golden hues,
Silly thoughts, and sticky shoes.
Fruits of joy in sunlit spray,
Chasing dreams, we laugh and play.

With every bite, the laughter spills,
Juicy tales beneath the hills.
Tickling taste buds, oh what fun!
Summer's magic has begun.

A dance of flavors in the air,
Sticky fingers everywhere.
Yummy giggles, wild and free,
Fruit catastrophe—joy, you see!

So grab a slice, don't make it neat,
Savor bliss in summer's heat.
Life's a feast that never ends,
With cheeky smiles and fruity friends.

When Twilight Meets the Orchard

As twilight hues begin to glow,
In orchards ripe, we laugh and flow.
Whispered jokes in fruit-laden boughs,
   Twinkling stars—oh, take a bow!

The laughter floats on evening breeze,
   Fruitful dreams post twilight tease.
   A mango slips, oh what a sight!
   Rolling round in evening light.

With giggles sparking in the trees,
   Sweetness swaying in the leaves.
   Nature's jest, a playful rhyme,
Harvesting laughs from dusk till prime.

So gather 'round, the fun begins,
   In sticky joy, we lose our sins.
   Under stars, so bright and grand,
Orchards bloom with humor planned.

Lush Dreams and Fruits Divine

In gardens lush, where laughter grows,
Fruits divine with cheeky prose.
A jester's dance in every tree,
Sprouting joy as sweet as can be.

With banana peels, we slip and slide,
Fruit confetti, oh what a ride!
Grinning apples in the sun,
Life's rich banquet, just for fun.

Grapes like giggles roll on ground,
Juicy whispers all around.
Lemons acting sour, so sly,
Making us laugh until we cry.

So raise a toast to trees of glee,
Where every fruit has a story.
In delightful slips and fruity rhymes,
We find our joy in silly times.

From Pulp to Poetic Heart

From juicy pulp, our hearts take flight,
With every bite, the world feels right.
Silly seeds of laughter sown,
Crafting joy when we dine alone.

Peaches roll like giggly dreams,
In sunlit lanes with funny themes.
Merry melodies in orchard's tune,
Jokes as sweet as pink-hued moon.

With every peel, humor's near,
Sticky laughter is what we cheer.
Fragrant moments, silly art,
We find pure joy within the heart.

So take a slice and pass it round,
In fruity bliss, let laughter sound.
Life's a poem, ripe and sweet,
With every taste, we're in for a treat.

Enchanted Orchard

In a grove where laughter sways,
Fruits dance in the sunny rays.
Mangoes chat with cheeky glee,
Winking at the bumblebee.

Squirrels juggle, nuts in hand,
While birds on branches take their stand.
A fruit mustache, oh what a sight,
Tropical giggles take flight.

The sun's a joker, bright and bold,
Casting shadows, stories told.
A splash of juice, a funny splash,
As ripe fruit drops in a sweet crash.

Lemons laugh at oranges' plight,
As they dance into the night.
In this orchard, joy runs wild,
Nature's laughter, sweetly styled.

Yoga of the Palms

In sunlit stretches, palms do sway,
Practicing their fun all day.
A mango's pose, a twist so neat,
Leaves shout, "Check this fancy feat!"

Lemons giggle in downward dog,
While coconuts roll like a fog.
A pineapple's tree pose, hold tight,
Wobble and dance 'til the night.

Bananas chant in meditative bliss,
Finding juiciness they can't miss.
Tree trunks creak with a hearty laugh,
Watching fruit take its silly path.

As the sun sinks low with flair,
Each fruit finds a comfy chair.
In this yoga, joy's the aim,
Flexibility is the game.

Beyond the Palate

In a kitchen full of delightful sights,
A mango plays in culinary fights.
With spoons and forks in a sneaky chase,
Each bite brings a funny face.

Avocado grins with creamy pride,
While spicy peppers dance beside.
A fruit salad, a colorful mix,
Stirring joy with each tasty fix.

Bananas slip on a joking peel,
Fruit thoughts that are certainly surreal.
A citrus burst leads to a cheer,
As laughter simmers, oh so near.

Desserts with sprinkles and silly names,
Each plateful, a silly game.
Taste the giggles, savor the cheer,
Food's a party, loud and clear!

A Journey in Citrus

A trip through orange groves so bright,
With lemons laughing at the sight.
A citrus train that rolls with zest,
Chugging along, it's simply the best.

Limes are sprinters, quick on toes,
Zipping past with funny prose.
Grapefruits giggle, pink and round,
In this circus, joy abound.

Citrus twists with a playful grin,
Juicing up laughs from deep within.
Sours and sweets in a wacky race,
Each tangy moment, a funny space.

Under the sun, a bright parade,
Where citrus dreams are surely made.
Join the journey, the laughter flows,
In this fruity land, anything goes.

Mango Serenades

In a tree, so high, I spy,
Mangoes dancing, oh my!
They twirl like stars in the night,
A fruity ballet, pure delight.

With a wink, they tease and sway,
Calling me to join their play,
I grab a spoon, and take my stance,
Join the mangoes in their dance!

Laughter bubbles, sweet and bright,
Juices streaming, what a sight!
With every bite, a giggle flows,
Mangoes burst, everyone knows!

I'll wear my mango hat with flair,
Waving to folks passing there,
"Come join the fun!" I shout with glee,
In this mango world, wild and free!

Shadows of Sweetness

A shadow stirs beneath the sun,
Mango mischief has begun!
They plot and scheme in the breeze,
Whispering secrets among the trees.

"Let's roll down this hill," they grin,
A fruity race, let's begin!
They tumble over, squishy and round,
Laughter erupts, such joy is found.

One mango shouts, "I'm the best!"
"Not if we drop, you'll fail this test!"
With every bump, they squeal with cheer,
As the world spins, we're all so near.

The shadows dance, the sun shines bright,
Mango capers in pure delight,
As evening falls, they stick in pairs,
Dreaming of sweetness and playful cares.

Citrine Wishes

Under the golden sunlit skies,
Mangoes wink, with gleaming eyes,
They whisper dreams of zesty fun,
"Come chase us all, run, run, run!"

With every hop and silly dash,
Mangoes giggle, make a splash,
They're off to the market, oh what a run,
Buying laughs, and just a ton!

A mango stepped up, proud and bold,
"I'm the sweetest, or so I'm told!"
But the others just roll their eyes,
"Your tales of sweetness are full of lies!"

In the end, with laughter shared,
Mangoes unite; none are spared,
Wishes float like clouds above,
In citrine delight, we find our love.

Blossoms of Memory

In the yard, memories bloom,
Mango trees spell out a tune,
Nostalgic whispers in the air,
Sweetness lingers everywhere.

We'd climb to heights, just like the birds,
Sharing tales without the words,
Each mango plucked was a delight,
Under the stars, every night.

Now we chuckle at those days,
Sipping nectar in carefree ways,
Laughter echoes, a sunny cheer,
Blossoms of memories, oh so dear!

A banquet served on leaves of green,
Silly stories woven between,
In every bite, we find the past,
Sweet mango dreams forever last!

Casting Shadows Amidst Fruit

In a garden lush and bright,
Lemons laugh, they take flight.
Bananas slip with easy grace,
While apples juggle in the race.

Grapes are gossiping in lines,
Chortling over fruit-inspired signs.
Coconuts don hats of style,
Inviting all to stay a while.

Laughter echoes through the trees,
As tangerines dance in the breeze.
Pineapples wear sunglasses low,
Life's a party, don't you know?

In this patch where joy is found,
Every fruit's a merry sound.
Here, whimsy rides on every vine,
Casting shadows, all divine!

Harvesting Dreams under Stars

Beneath a sky of twinkling lights,
Fruits conspire on starry nights.
Peaches whisper dreams so sweet,
While cherries trip on tiny feet.

Ripe mangoes laugh, they roll away,
Playing games until the day.
Jellybeans join in the fun,
Bouncing freely, one by one.

Dreamers come to share a tale,
With juicy bites that never fail.
Kiwis bask in all the cheer,
With gummy worms as honored seer.

Underneath those shining beams,
Harvesting all of our wild dreams.
Happiness drips from every crop,
As stars wink and never stop!

The Glow of Ripening Joy

In orchards bright where laughter grows,
Fruit sings songs nobody knows.
Watermelons wear grins so wide,
As lemons tease from the other side.

Berries bounce and play a tune,
While sunbeams dance beneath the moon.
Juicy jokes are served on plates,
With all the fun that brightly rates.

Oranges twirl like ballerinas,
In a world of fruit-filled arenas.
Mirth ripens with every day,
Turning simple dreams to play.

Joy spills over, oh so grand,
As fruits unite in merry band.
With every cheerful little bite,
Life's a feast of pure delight!

Where Dreams and Sunshine Meet

In a world where fruits can talk,
Lemons laugh, and radishes walk.
Grapefruits wear their favorite shoes,
In colors that even rainbows choose.

Citrus suns smile down with glee,
Crafting giggles from each tree.
Let's toast to grapes in fizzy streams,
As we bubble up our dreams.

With every harvest, joy expands,
While cantaloupes hold out their hands.
Where sunshine meets our merry cheer,
Life's a carnival, have no fear!

So raise your glass to all things fine,
As fruits and dreams together shine.
In this garden where we play,
Laughter blooms every day!

Essence of Juicy Reverie

In gardens green where visions bloom,
A fruit so bright dispels all gloom.
With laughter shared and bites of cheer,
We chase the sun, our joy sincere.

The trees wear crowns of golden delight,
As giggles burst like stars at night.
With each sweet taste, our spirits take flight,
In fantasies wrapped, the world feels right.

Oh, sticky hands and silly grins,
We play like kids, where laughter spins.
A fruity feast, our hearts align,
In this bizarre, yet joyful dine.

A symphony of squishy fun,
As friendships grow beneath the sun.
With every slice, a tale is spun,
In juicy joys, we've just begun.

Dreaming in Golden Hues

A burst of yellow, dreams so bold,
In every bite, a tale retold.
We giggle as we lick our lips,
In sunny days, the laughter skips.

With friends around, we share the thrill,
Each juicy drop gives hearts a chill.
In sticky sweets, our worries fade,
In summer's glow, our plans are made.

The shadows dance beneath the trees,
As fruit falls gently in the breeze.
A tasty mess, oh what a sight,
We find our joy in pure delight.

In dreaming realms where colors blend,
We raise our cups, let laughter mend.
For every seed and every scoop,
We celebrate our quirky troupe.

Serenade of Sweetness

With each sweet morsel, hearts arise,
A serenade beneath the skies.
The laughter bubbles, joy expands,
As fruity wonders fill our hands.

In silly games, we toss in cheer,
A fruity fight that draws us near.
With smiles like sunshine, we unite,
In this delightful, silly plight.

Oh, drippy smiles and sugary plays,
We dance through all those golden days.
With every bite, our spirits soar,
We relish life, forevermore.

The sweetness sings, the summer calls,
In vibrant hues, our laughter sprawls.
So here we stand, with joy unbarred,
In this fun-filled world, we've truly starred.

Echoes of a Summer Fruit

In whispers soft, the fruit does sway,
As laughter echoes through the day.
With every chuckle, joy persists,
In this bright world, we can't resist.

The tales we weave of sticky fun,
Are woven deep beneath the sun.
As we indulge in sweet delight,
Our spirits dance, our hearts take flight.

Oh, shades of warmth in every taste,
We relish life, not one bit waste.
With glee and giggles, we embark,
In fruity realms, we leave our mark.

For every bite, a memory forms,
In silly shouts as joy transforms.
In summer's light, the world is bright,
Together, we laugh into the night.

Embrace of the Season

In a land where the sun always smiles,
Fruit falls like jokes from the sky.
Laughter mingles with sweet, juicy spills,
Nature's jest is never shy.

Wandering through hues of bright yellow,
Sipping on nectar, a sticky delight.
Each bite brings a giggle, a cheer,
The flavor of fun, pure and light.

Birds join in with their chattering songs,
While squirrels dance to the rhythm of glee.
Nature's a stage for the silly and fun,
In a world where we're all wild and free.

Vibrant Visions

A canvas painted in colors so bold,
With bursts of laughter and mischievous glee.
Fruits plump and juicy with stories untold,
Each taste a secret, a sweet mystery.

The wind winks as it plays with my hair,
Tickling my senses, a playful spree.
Life's a parade of flavors to share,
With each little nibble, it's pure jubilee.

In this orchard of dreams, we skip and we sing,
Chasing shadows of blossoms that sway.
With a twirl and a laugh, we embrace the spring,
In vibrant colors, let's frolic and play.

Symphony of the Earth

Hear the giggles of leaves in the breeze,
As fruits fall like notes from a high-flying bird.
Nature composes humorous melodies,
While we hum along, feeling absurd.

The grass whispers jokes as we tumble with glee,
Crickets chirp in a comedic twist.
Laughter's the thread that binds you and me,
In this grand, earthy, uproarious tryst.

Dancing under the sun, silly and wild,
Every shadow has something to say.
Unruly and free, just like a child,
In this symphony, let's play the day.

Nuances of Nature

In the orchard of whimsy, fruits giggle and play,
With a wink and a burst, they topple and roll.
They tease like old friends on a bright, sunny day,
Sprinkling joy like confetti in a bowl.

Each leaf tells a story, a pun or a jest,
A world full of humor, where laughter's the key.
Nature's paintbrush strokes hues of the best,
In a gallery of fun, come wander with me.

With a sip of the nectar, we dance in our dreams,
Twisting and swirling in laughter's embrace.
The season is bright, or so it seems,
Nurtured by nature's comical grace.

Orchard of Delights

In the trees, a wobbly fruit,
Swinging low, just like a hoot.
Buzzing bees in a busy trance,
Dancing round in a silly dance.

Bright yellow glories in the sun,
They're so ripe, it looks like fun.
Underfoot, the squishy mess,
Oh, who knew fruit could cause such stress!

Squirrels plotting with a cheeky grin,
They'll swipe my snack if I'm not in!
Laughing hard at their silly heist,
It's a party that's oh-so-nice.

With every bite, a squirt of bliss,
Who can resist such fruity kiss?
In this place, we're all just kids,
Living life without a squids!

Beyond the Orchard's Gate

Sneaky jays with a flashy flair,
Eyeing fruit without a care.
They'll swoop down and grab a round,
In this chase, I'm seldom found.

Footsteps soft on the grassy trail,
Searching out that sweet, sweet grail.
Oh, the giggles as I slip and slide,
Into sticky puddles, I can't hide!

Gangs of friends with the sticky hands,
Eating fruit like rockstar bands.
Chasing shadows, we run wild,
Crazy antics of a joyful child.

At dusk, we laugh and reminisce,
About the day and all its bliss.
Under stars, we dream and scheme,
In our world, it's still a dream!

Sweet Escapades

Morning sun and skies so blue,
Under trees where laughter grew.
Swinging low, a perfect day,
With my pals, we laugh and play.

A mango falls, it rolls away,
We're hot on its tail, what a fray!
Trip and tumble, giggling spree,
Nature's playground, wild and free.

Wipe the juice from cheeky grins,
This ripe delight, where mischief wins.
Kick the seeds like little balls,
In this game, nobody stalls!

Sunset paints the skies with gold,
Stories shared, and laughter bold.
Dreaming of our next crusade,
In this orchard, friendships made.

Tropical Fantasia

Colorful fruits and fruity cheer,
Bouncing smiles as we draw near.
Crazy colors, yellow and green,
It's the wildest sight I've seen!

We build castles from the fruit,
Jelly walls and a jelly brute.
Squishy floors make us laugh, oh dear!
Twist of fate, we're stuck right here!

Just watch out for the fallen peels,
Bouncing back are our squealing heels.
With each slip comes a world of fun,
Laughter echoes as we run!

Underneath the palm tree shade,
We munch our treasures, still afraid.
That tomorrow, with all its glee,
Brings more adventures, just you and me!

Heartbeats in the Mangroves

In the shade of tangled trees,
A lizard charms with clumsy ease.
Chasing dreams of flying high,
He just trips and shakes his thigh.

Beneath the leaves, a couple dance,
Twisting limbs in rising trance.
They drop their snacks, what a sight!
A mango rolls, oh what delight!

Frogs croak tunes of love and cheer,
While fish jump high, not in fear.
Nature's laughter fills the air,
Where silly antics match the flair.

Yet, through these mangroves, dreams do blend,
A world of joy that won't soon end.
With every heartbeat, laughs will bloom,
In this embrace, there's always room.

Finding Solace in Sunset's Glow

As daylight fades, the colors play,
A golden stretch at end of day.
The sun dips low, the sky in swoon,
While crickets start their silly tune.

A pie of fruit, the ants decide,
To feast upon, oh what a ride!
With sticky hands and happy grins,
They trip and slip; who really wins?

The clouds burst forth with orange flair,
While fireflies dance in evening air.
Each spark a thought, both light and brief,
Their funny games bring sweet relief.

So let the sunset be our guide,
With laughter rolling like the tide.
In glowing hues, our spirits lift,
In nature's gift, we find our gift.

Dreams Adrift in Citrus Clouds

Up in the sky, a fruit parade,
With citrus orbs that can't evade.
A flying lemon screams with glee,
As oranges dance like waves at sea.

A grapefruit tries to spin and twirl,
While limes just bounce and give a whirl.
With every twist, they giggle loud,
Creating dreams within the cloud.

Juggling joy, they slip and fall,
A zesty laugh, embracing all.
They bounce right back, it's plain to see,
In this bright world, they're wild and free.

Citrus wishes take to flight,
In joyful chaos, pure delight.
Across the sky, they let dreams bloom,
In citrus clouds, there's always room.

A Journey through Ripe Realms

In fields of gold, where laughter grows,
A charming breeze brings giggles close.
With ripe delights around they roam,
Each fruit, a friend, feels just like home.

With careful steps, a mischief brews,
A berry rolls away, just to choose.
It hops along to tease and play,
While others cheer, 'Hip-hip-hooray!'

Now ripe realms twist and spin with cheer,
Bananas giggle, 'Here, come near!'
They sway and trip in dazzling light,
While melons boast, 'We're out of sight!'

So join the chase through nature's hue,
Where joy can spark and antics stew.
In every bite and laugh shared wide,
Adventure blooms, let's take that ride.

Whispers of Juicy Days

In a tree high above, sat a fruit with glee,
It called out, 'Hey buddy, come sit with me!'
With a squish and a splat, juice dripped on the ground,
All around would laugh, what a sticky surround!

The squirrels conspired, they plotted and played,
How to snag sweetness, they'd never be swayed.
One slipped and he flopped, bounced like a small bean,
When the laughter erupted, you'd think he was seen!

There's joy in the pit, if one can look right,
Between chaos and sweetness, oh what a delight!
With every ripe bite, a giggle escapes,
In a world full of fruit, we all wear funny capes!

So gather your friends, let the munching commence,
For fun's in the feast, it's all pure nonsense.
In the shade of the tree, tales twist and entwine,
Living large on the juice, oh how life can shine!

Reflections on a Mango Breeze

Beneath a blue sky, where laughter unfurls,
A fruit that can dance, with a whirl and a twirl.
With the breeze on its cheeks and a wink in its skin,
It teases the taste buds of all who come in.

A fellow named Joe took a big, silly bite,
From a fruit so bright, it lit up the night.
With laughter erupting, juice splattered around,
You'd think he was dancing on sweet, fruity ground!

As birds chirped their songs, crickets joined the beat,
The funky old farmer sat back in his seat.
He winked at the fruit, 'You're quite the charmer!'
While the fruit grinned back, sippin' juice like a farmer.

So here's to the moments, so juicy and bold,
Dancing under the sun, never getting too old.
In a world ripe with laughter, where dreams chase the breeze,
Life's better with laughter, and mango-scented trees!

Fields of Flavor

In the fields where flavors frolic and play,
A fruit rolls along, chasing sunshine all day.
With a bounce and a giggle, it leaps like a sprite,
Squirrels chase after, what a silly sight!

'Come pluck me!' it sings, dancing under the sun,
Where shadows make friends, and the laughter is fun.
Each bite is a riddle, a burst of delight,
Sweet nectar in laughter, oh what a height!

The grass whispers tales of the jokes that they've known,
Of fruits that have tumbled, and seeds they have sown.
With only good vibes and a splash of pure cheer,
Fields filled with flavor, where joy is sincere!

So wander these meadows, take a bite, share the fun,
Where flavors collide, every heart leaves as one.
In the fields of flavor, life dances to the tune,
You'll be laughing for hours, 'neath the mango moon!

Orgasmic Hues of Twilight

When the sun starts to dip, and the sky turns to gold,
A fruit in the twilight feels daring and bold.
With colors so bright, like a sunset's embrace,
It giggles and wiggles, a whimsical grace!

From yellow to orange, then red, what a sight,
It's the life of the party, all day and all night.
With every new hue, it teases and plays,
Inviting the moon to join in the frays.

The creatures all gather, it's a fruity soirée,
From dawn until dusk, they dive right in the fray.
With laughter and zest, they take up the dance,
A riot of colors, oh what a chance!

So here's to the twilight, that laughter-filled scene,
Where juicy delights are forever our queen.
With flavors exploding, oh what a delight,
In the hues of the night, we find pure, fruity light!

Nectar of the Gods

In the grove where laughter spills,
Golden fruits do dance on hills.
A bite reveals a splash of cheer,
Sticky fingers bring good fortune here.

Sipping juice on sunny days,
Bees buzzing in a happy craze.
Mangoes whisper sweet delight,
Wishing every day was bright.

Friends gather for a fruity feast,
The mess we make, a joyful beast.
Seeds like treasure, we forget to chomp,
But giggles roll and can't be stopped.

So let us feast beneath the sun,
With every slice, we share the fun.
For in this grove, we find our bliss,
A silly dream, oh how we miss!

Sun-Kissed Soliloquy

A mango's wink from branches high,
Beneath the shade, we can't deny.
With laughter bubbling in the air,
Who knew fruit could create such flair?

We prance and play like silly cows,
Discussing life and fruit and how.
In the sun, we share our whims,
Each juicy bite makes our hearts brim.

The juice drips down in a rhythm sweet,
We dance and twirl, our barefeet greet.
Sticky smiles and goofy slips,
While mango dreams dance on our lips.

As shadows stretch and day bows low,
Under the trees, our laughter flows.
With fruit in hand, we own the joy,
Life's fruity game, no one can choy!

Papery Skies and Tender Eyes

In clouds of fluff where dreams reside,
Echoed giggles, we won't hide.
Papery skies whisper tales of bliss,
A feast of fruit, who could resist?

Beneath the branches, tales take flight,
With lovers' laughter, all is right.
A splash of juice, a dash of zest,
We savor life, it's simply the best.

Tender eyes gleam, a secret peek,
As juicy treasures make us squeak.
With every squirt, our souls ignite,
In this fruity game, we delight.

And when the sun dips down to play,
We gather all our socks and sway.
For in this whimsied, fruity spree,
We find together, oh so free!

A Dream Beneath Canopy

Under leaves where sunlight streams,
Laughter mingles with our dreams.
Mangoes sway in playful tease,
Nature's bounty puts us at ease.

Sipping nectar, sticky and sweet,
Sharing tales that none can beat.
With splattered clothes and sunny smiles,
We build our memories in silly styles.

The canopy holds our joyful screams,
As we tumble through our fruity themes.
Lost in sweetness, hearts collide,
A joyful escapade, side by side.

With twilight creeping in soft embrace,
We gather reflections from this place.
In dreams below the leafy sways,
We find our laughter never decays!

The Scent of Elysium

In a grove where laughter grows,
Mangoes dance in sunny rows.
Each bite bursts with giggles sweet,
A comical tang, a fruity treat.

Wily peels like jester's hats,
Rolling laughter, like sneaky cats.
Juice drips down like summer rain,
Tickling taste buds, joy unchained.

Sunshine wraps like a warm embrace,
In every slice, a silly face.
Tropical breezes play a tune,
As mango dreams keep hearts in bloom.

So let us dance on this ripe spree,
With sticky fingers, wild and free.
In every mango, a joke it seems,
Whimsical moments, simple dreams.

Summer's Tender Embrace

Underneath this blazing sun,
Mangoes gleam, oh what fun!
Each one's laughter, a juicy squish,
A humorous tale, a delicious wish.

Sticky smiles, a fruity feast,
Belly laughs, the laughter's beast.
Gulping slices, hearts aglow,
As friends unite, and good vibes flow.

In the shade, we share a bite,
Sun-kissed faces, pure delight.
Sweetness drips, we're in a jam,
While bees buzz by to join our clan.

With careless giggles, we declare,
Nothing's better, it's all laid bare.
In mango moments, joy ignites,
A summer's love, our hearts take flights.

In the Company of Leaves

Among the branches, green and bright,
Mango dreams take joyful flight.
Swinging branches, playful sway,
As leaves whisper secrets of the day.

Squirrels giggle, watch us eat,
Juicy treasures, oh so sweet.
With every munch, we burst in glee,
In this fruity world, we're wild and free.

Silly shadows dance and play,
With each splash of golden ray.
Laughter surely fills the air,
As mangoes bring us joy to share.

Take a bite, let worries cease,
In the company of leaves, we find peace.
With every juicy, silly flash,
Life unfolds in a laughter dash.

Musings of a Juicy Day

What a day! Oh, what a sight,
Mangoes gleaming, pure delight.
In each slice, a tale unique,
With every chew, the world's a freak.

Sun so bright, like a jester's grin,
With juicy drips, we laugh within.
The clock's a joke, it ticks away,
In this fruity frenzy, we choose to stay.

Belly's full of laughter sweet,
As sunshine dances on our feet.
Life's a feast, a playful spree,
In juicy musings, we're all carefree.

So let us taste this silly play,
In every mango, a sunny ray.
Our hearts are light, our spirits sway,
In musings of a juicy day.

Lush Aromas and Daydreams

In a grove where fruits reside,
Sweet scents dance, play, and glide.
The bees hum tunes, they find their way,
While chomping on dreams every sunny day.

Beneath the trees, the laughter spills,
As juice runs down from playful thrills.
One bite in, the giggles swell,
A fruit-filled tale that weaves so well.

Shadows play, and colors swirl,
With every bite, a giggly twirl.
In this land where wonders beam,
Life tastes brighter; it's a dream!

Oh! The sticky fingers we all boast,
Each drop a win, we love the most.
In laughter's midst, we're children still,
With wild imaginations, there's time to fill.

A Slice of Paradise

A round, bright orb with golden glow,
It winks at me, 'Come on, let's go!'
With every slice, I'm taken far,
To sunlit shores, beneath a star.

Juicy drips down chins of cheer,
We giggle loud; our joy is clear.
Each munch a tickle, a fruity jest,
In this paradise, we're truly blessed.

Sun hats and shades, our fashion true,
With patterns bright and vibrant hue.
We're dancing round with no care,
In a fruit-bowl world, without a snare.

Sweetened laughs and playful grins,
A slice of joy, where fun begins.
Oh, take a seat and join the cheer,
In this fruity realm, it's all sincere!

Dancing with Dappled Light

In the dappled sun, we find our muse,
With fruity giggles we can't refuse.
Twirling 'round, dreams take their flight,
As shadows sway, our hearts ignite.

Beneath the boughs, it's just pure fun,
With nature's laughter, we become one.
Fruity melodies fill the air,
With every taste, we lose our care.

Land of fizz, with flavors bright,
A taste of joy that feels just right.
We prance and skip, and play around,
In a world where giggles abound.

The sun dips low; the day wears thin,
Yet in our hearts, the laughter spins.
A fruity ballet, wild and free,
In the dance of light, we find glee.

Ripe Visions

Visions ripen on the tree,
Each plump treasure calls to me.
With cheeky grins and sugar bliss,
In this fruity world, who could resist?

The branch bows low, inviting all,
Jump up high; let's make the call!
To splash, to dash, in sweet delight,
Where every moment feels just right.

Laughter bursts like bubbles sweet,
As we dance on sugar feet.
With each full bite and playful glance,
In this grand orchard, let's all prance!

The twilight glows, the stars peek through,
In this ripe dream, we're meant to stew.
With fruity joy, we are alive,
In a world where happy dreams thrive.

The Dreamer's Harvest

In a garden where the rice sings,
Mangoes dangle like bright gold rings.
A ladder sways, my heart it zings,
I reach up high for nature's flings.

But on that step, my foot does slip,
I tumble down, oh what a trip!
A mango flies, with a joyful flip,
It lands on me with a juicy drip.

I sit and laugh amidst the fruits,
Sticky fingers in my boots.
Every bite gives sweet reboots,
I dance around in joyful hoots.

The sun sets low with a wink, so fine,
Mango juice becomes my wine.
With sticky hands, I feel divine,
Harvesting dreams from this tree of mine.

Whims of the Summer Wind

The summer breeze tells laughter's tale,
Whipping fruits off the branch, they sail.
Chasing mangoes, oh what a trail,
A sweet pursuit, I cannot fail.

A fuzzy friend, a cheeky bee,
Flies by my ear, just teasing me.
While I chase down the fruity spree,
It zooms away—too fast, you see!

With sticky toes and fumbled moves,
I dart and dodge, my body grooves.
Nature's game, it always proves,
Life's more fun in silly hooves.

As night comes in, stars take their place,
Mango scents float, a soft embrace.
Summer winds dance in a wacky race,
The world spins round with a funny face.

Bliss Amongst Branches

In leafy arms, where sweetness grows,
I spy a mango, it brightly glows.
With playful leaps, my garden knows,
Joy acts up as excitement flows.

A jump, a twist, a swing so grand,
I snag the fruit, it's close at hand.
But who knew that my luck was planned?
Down goes the mango, it lands—thud! On sand!

With giggling friends, we scoop and munch,
Sunshine laughter—oh, what a bunch!
Each fruity bite—a juicy crunch,
In our own world, we form a punch.

As birds chuckle, the day drifts near,
We splash and play, with nary a fear.
In nature's belly, there's cheer to steer,
Bliss among branches, we love to cheer.

Lively Days in the Orchard

In an orchard where the sun does shine,
Lively fruit dangles from the vine.
Mango madness, oh how divine,
With giggles and grins, we intertwine.

I grab a mango, feel its weight,
But little did I know—oh fate!
It rolls away, oh what a state,
Chasing it down, I can't be late.

With silly antics, we run and play,
Dancing dodges in a feisty ballet.
Every twist reminds me to say,
Life's a joke—come out and sway!

As twilight settles and stars align,
We feast on dreams, fruit on the fine.
Lively days, with bliss entwined,
In these moments, true joy we find.

www.ingramcontent.com/pod-product-compliance
Lightning Source LLC
Chambersburg PA
CBHW060144230426
43661CB00003B/569